T0365823

GARDEN
Ideas
from DAD

PHILLIP H. SMITH

AuthorHouse™
1663 Liberty Drive
Bloomington, IN 47403
www.authorhouse.com
Phone: 1-800-839-8640

Published by AuthorHouse 03/24/2015

ISBN: 978-1-4969-5060-4 (sc)
ISBN: 978-1-4969-5061-1 (e)

Print information available on the last page.

This book is printed on acid-free paper.

authorHOUSE®

Contents

ABOUT THE AUTHOR

Phil Smith is a member of various garden organizations and has been a gardener since he was eight years old. He was born in Hartford City, Indiana, in 1936 and obtained his engineering degree at Purdue University in 1956 at age 20. He then earned a J D (Doctor of Jurisprudence) law degree at Indiana University in 1959. Mr. Smith specialized in trademark law in Minneapolis with the firm of Merchant, Gould, Smith and Edell, now known as Merchant & Gould. He wrote the law book Intent-To-Use Trademark Practice published in 1992 by BNA Books.

Because of his interest in gardening and plant terminology, Mr. Smith wrote and prosecuted several U.S. Plant Patents. The most well known is Plant Patent 7,197 on the Honeycrisp apple which was developed by the University of Minnesota.

Phil Smith had extensive flower gardens at the home of he and his first wife Anne on Coolidge Ave in St. Louis Park. Quite a few years later, Phil and his second wife Wanda had a home in the Tyroll Hills subdivision of Golden Valley, and Phil had large flower gardens there. The writer retired at age 57 and then he and Wanda lived in Montana in the summer and Florida in the winter. Phil's gardens in Golden Valley were on tours most summers, sometimes by nation-wide groups.

The author has been a member of the Mens Garden Club of Minneapolis (now known as the Mens and Women's Garden Club of Minneapolis) for over 50 years, and he also served as President of the Minnesota State Horticultural Society in 1973 and 1974. Phil was one of the founders of the Minnesota Landscape Arboretum and was the first chair of their Board of Directors. Also, for several years he was the U.S. Vice-President of the Delphinium Society headquartered in England. The primary interests of the author are perennials and the design of flower borders with numerous varieties.

ABOUT THIS BOOK

The author wishes to note that all the photos included in this book are photos taken of the author's various gardens, except for the two photos on page 50 of the Koopmans' garden in Faribault, Minnesota.

With respect to the plants reviewed in this book and the author's recommendations on plant culture, we will generally be considering plant culture in climates north of the mid temperatures between the Gulf of Mexico and Canada. This does not refer to a straight line east to west across mid America, since temps change with elevations. Although I have never gardened in Canada, I assume this would include the southern areas of our northern neighbor, as well as southern areas in the U.S. which have higher elevations.

As a precaution, I wish to remind people that various plants may be poisonous to taste, and for some people to touch, so children in particular should be cautioned.

The photo below and the photos on next two pages show some features of the author's garden in Golden Valley, Minnesota.

DESIGNING FLOWER BORDERS

The term "border" is a garden term often used in Great Britain. To me it primarily means a garden at the back or sides of a property or a garden bordering an expanse of lawn. The plant varieties used may depend on the space, the available depth of the garden, and the preferences of the gardener. If enough space is available, a border may feature some flowering shrubs in the background, fronted by a framework of hardy perennials and highlighted with some colorful annuals. I sometimes include spring bulbs, over which may be planted summer annuals.

A favorite design of the writer is a long sweeping curve at the front of the border, with a teardrop shape at one end. Another pleasing feature is to place some evergreens or shrubs at the end of one section, such as at the middle or end of a side yard garden, to partially block the next area. With this design, when one reaches the end and the beginning of the next area, there is the surprise of a new view to behold.

With respect to edgings, I like to use one color of an annual to line the front edge of a border, such as alyssum, fibrous begonias, or other dwarf plants. However, if a landscape has significant changes in elevation, it may be nice to construct the border like a raised bed with a low retaining wall in front. This also provides good drainage. As for dimensions, I prefer at least ten feet in depth to design a nice border. Otherwise, perhaps just a planting of shrubs or perhaps a specialty grouping, such a hostas or annuals, will suffice. When deciding how to arrange the desired plants, the general idea is to place the taller types (such as delphiniums, foxglove, monkshood) in back, intermediate heights in mid range and more dwarf varieties in front. However, I will occasionally place a highlight feature in the front area by inserting a taller perennial as a special display.

Gardeners sometimes work hard to achieve a desired color arrangement, such as yellows with blues and purple, reds with pink or orange, blues with whites, etc. However, I normally follow just one rule, and that is to include a generous amount of white, which sets off the other colors.

Doing this seems to let the other color arrangements generally work without much effort in laying out color patterns. Sometimes we read about gardens with all the various plants being all the same color. I will always cherish the all-white garden at Sissinghurst Castle in England. It has for many years been my dream to design and plant such a garden but to date have not yet got it done.

PERENNIAL BORDERS AND TOOL SHED

The photos below show portions of my previous borders in St. Louis Park, Mn, including the garden tool shed I designed and built.

As to spacing and grouping of plants, I like to use groupings of three or five of the same species, depending on size, and spaced according to the variety. For example, I would space delphiniums in the background about three feet apart, but a grouping of aquilegia or dianthus near the front might be spaced about 12 inches apart.

Perennials in northern states sometimes do not survive a hard winter, despite best efforts at drainage and covering. Some loose covering is usually desired, but sometimes with a wet spring the soggy covering may do more damage than good. This is one reason why it is nice to have a nursery area in the back of your garden and grow some perennials each year from seed. The gardener will then have a supply of plants each year to replace those lost to winter conditions. Spaces can also be filled with plantings of colorful annuals, which I sometimes plant in "drifts" of several plants of the same color in one area.

The planting of a so-called mixed border emphasizes the need to prepare the soil well when the border is first constructed. Use of gypsum and lots of organic material is highly beneficial. Gypsum is a calcium sulfate product and very useful for breaking down clay soil. I also consider calcium to be number four in the group of nutrients required by plants, that is nitrogen, phosphate, potash and calcium.

When a mixed border is planted, it is of course not possible to spade over the soil each year, unless one removes all the perennials. This is of course not practical. Accordingly, what one can do is spread some gypsum and a layer of organic material in the open spaces between the perennials, and dig over the soil in the spaces around all the perennials. When living in Minnesota, I preferred to do this chore in the autumn so the soil would mellow with the freezing and thawing over the winter.

The design and layout of a flower border is highly personal in nature, and the rules can sometimes be ignored in favor of personal preferences. Just do not expect your efforts to be magazine perfect right after planting. One pleasing benefit of gardening is the chance to be creative.

SOIL PREPARATION

Most gardeners know that soil preparation and conditioning are one of the most important elements for successful gardening. This is something I learned from my grandmother when I was a young and it has been good advice which I always try to follow. When moving to a new home I have occasionally used a cultivator over the ground and planted some annuals for a little first year color when there was not time to really prepare the soil. However, the results were never very satisfying.

My sincere recommendation is to hand dig the garden area with either a sharp shovel or strong fork. I prefer to dig approximately 12 inches deep which I like to do for a nice garden. Most cultivators only churn the soil about three inches deep and are best used in veggie gardens where there are row crops. After the soil has once been hand dug deeply, a cultivator may be used in later years for veggie gardens to mix in compost and prepare the soil for planting, as well as for weed control between the rows of crops.

In a mixed border where there are numerous perennials to cherish from year to year, a cultivator is not appropriate.

Double Digging

Until the last few years when my arthritic back and legs cannot take the work, I have always double dug the garden area the first year before planting. This is the old English method which I recommend for a garden which is to have perennials and be maintained for several years. Few people are willing to undertake the effort, and although it is a lot of work it is well worth the effort. Should a reader wish to do it for a special garden, this is the procedure for either bare soil or an area with grass. Starting at one end, dig a trench two shovel layers deep and wheelbarrow such removed soil to the other end of the plot. Then, dig and move the next trench top layer into the bottom of the first trench, mixing in some organic and gypsum. Next, dig the bottom layer of the next trench and move it to the top of the first trench, again with organic and gypsum. Proceed with the double layer digging all the way through the plot and use the hauled soil to finish off the far end. Best results are obtained if 3 to 4 inches of compost or organic and some gypsum are mixed in each of the two layers of trench soil. This method and various other techniques were taught to me many years ago by a neighbor who had immigrated from England to the U.S. when he was young.

As for digging tools, I favor a long handled shovel or a long handled heavy-duty fork. Long handles are much easier on the back. I prefer a long handled shovel or spade for digging the first year since it cuts easier through clay, sod and roots. However, if there are many rocks or other obstructions, a heavy fork is often easier to use. In later years when the soil has been worked, I prefer the fork since it seems to work quicker.

If one has a clay soil, it is very important to incorporate a lot of organic material (as much as 4 inches), as well as gypsum and perhaps some sand, before planting. Gypsum works to break down the clay. If the gardener uses quite a fair amount of gypsum, such as a bag per 150 sq. feet of garden, for two or three years, the heaviest clay soil will break down into a nice garden loam. Also, it is desirable to add 3 inches or so of organic material every year in the spring to each garden. I do so and dig it in, including around any existing perennials.

Where deciduous trees are common, the wet leaves which accumulate in the fall are a good source of organic. In some cities the leaves are hauled away in the autumn, composted over the winter, and made available in the spring to be picked up by gardeners. It is also a good idea to make your own compost bed if you have a decent source of leaves. Another very good source of organic is horse manure, although if fresh it should also be composted for a year.

STARTING FROM SEED

Growing plants from seed is an enjoyable and rewarding hobby and often an economical way to acquire larger numbers of plants at a lower cost than purchasing container grown plants. However, if one requires only a few plants of each variety, the cost of the seed and the time and effort involved may outweigh the simplicity of purchasing plants from a reliable source.

Some gardeners save a fair amount of money by growing from seed if they do it well. With the high cost of seed for the newer hybrids, it is desirable to use techniques which result in good germination and production of a high percentage of quality seedlings. Besides costs, another advantage of seeding is the ability to grow unusual or newer varieties which may not be available or are in short supply at garden centers.

Medium

Many varieties need only warmth and moisture to germinate, while others have further needs. Some may need darkness and others need good light, while some need cool temps and others temps of about 70. Also, other varieties may need to escape dormancy or have their hard coats broken. Sowing seeds successfully may require exactness and patience.

For a starting medium, you may purchase a good seed starting mix or make your own. A good mix is two parts good garden loam, one part clean sand, and one part peat moss or fine vermiculite. If the materials are dry, a wetting agent or some moisture will be needed. After filling the seeding pots, I like to take another pot or other object with a flat bottom and press the medium to form a smooth and even surface for sowing the seeds.

Fungus Diseases

For many growers, fungus diseases are the main problem in getting good germination. There are kinds which attack the seeds and prevent germination, and others referred to as "damp off" fungus which attack the seedlings after germination and cause them to wilt, rot and die. To prevent these problems, the medium may be sterilized by placing in a shallow pan, adding water if needed to make the medium damp, and baking for 45 minutes or so at 180 degrees F.

One of the best techniques for avoiding damp off is to always use about a half inch of milled sphagnum moss (which is sterile) on top of the medium. Seeds may also be coated with a small amount of fungicide powder by shaking in a small bottle or plastic baggy. Some growers always use distilled water for the medium and when watering the small seedlings, since tap water may likely carry some of the fungi.

Containers

Almost any container may be used for starting seedlings. Examples are flats, pots, plastic food trays, bottoms of milk cartons or jugs, egg cartons, etc. I prefer to use 4 inch plastic pots since they are easy to sterilize and to also cover to retain moisture before germination. You can also write the variety names on the side with a grease pencil or fine point permanent marker. To sterilize containers, most types may be washed in a solution of 2 tablespoons of household bleach per quart of water, and then rinsed.

Paper Towels

Pre-sprouting seeds in damp paper towels is an effective technique and particularly desirable for expensive seeds or those obtained from a rare source such as plant societies. The writer has had difficulty with this method for very tiny seeds such as begonias, but found the procedure effective for seeds requiring a longer germination period or being more susceptible to damp off. The specifics are to moisten two sheets of paper towels, lay one out flat on a surface and place the seeds in a pattern so that they are not touching. Place the other towel on top, roll up the towels and place in a clean plastic bag. If warmth is helpful for germination, which it is for many varieties, you can place the bag on top of the refrigerator. After a few days, check the seeds in the bag daily for germination, and when the seedlings get their first true leaves, it is time to promptly transplant the seeds into little pots or in rows in flats. They will be quite fragile so a delicate hand is required, especially for the tinier sprouts.

Temperature

Seeds of some genera desire warmth for germination, such as about 72 to 75 degrees F. The packets of seeds often give the desired temperature for germination. Gardeners who do a lot of seeding often use a germination chamber for those seeds requiring warmth, particular if the room where you do your seeding is not near this temp. A wood box may be used, with a 60 watt light bulb (or smaller depending on the box size) placed in the bottom of the box in a safe manner to not get wet or cause a fire, and a middle shelf upon which seed containers are placed.

The somewhat warm box will increase germination for varieties which prefer a warmer germination temp, but I do not want the box temp to be over 75 degrees F. A lid is required for seeds requiring darkness. Damp sphagnum moss may be placed around the pots in the box to prevent drying out.

Some perennials and woody plants desire coolness for germination. An example is delphiniums which are difficult to germinate above about 60 degrees F.

Dark or Light

Darkness for germination is required for some genera. Examples are delphiniums, phlox, nemesia, and many vegetables. To provide darkness, cover the pots or flats with plastic wrap and then add a magazine or some layers of newspaper. Some genera require light for germination, so for those the pots etc. should not be covered but placed in an area with good light but not direct sunlight. If the seeds are small, such as begonias, petunias and impatiens, do not cover but sow the seed directly on top of the medium. Some genera, particularly perennials, desire or may even require stratification for germination. That is, placing a layer of seeding medium on top of the seeds, the thickness of the medium or strata depending on the size of the seeds. Examples are acquilegia, dicentra, dictamus and hemerocallis. Stratification encourages the seeds to escape from dormancy. One procedure I sometimes use for seeds more difficult to germinate is to soak the seeds for a day in warm water (110 degrees F.), then mix with damp sand, place in a baggy and store in the refrigerator for about a month before germination.

Scarification

Some seeds have such a hard coating that moisture cannot penetrate or the cotyledons cannot break through, and such seeds must be scarified to germinate. Scarification of seeds means to cut or damage the shell of the seeds to permit the entry of moisture for germination. Examples of seeds requiring scarification are lupins, pansies, and sweet peas. Impatiens sometimes need the treatment but many seed companies now already do the treatment before marketing. Larger seeds may be scarified by nicking with a knife or rubbing with a file until the coat is broken is one spot along the seam or joint. This permits moisture to dampen the seeds. Small seeds are sometimes treated by soaking for 24 hours in warm water and then sown without drying out.

Seeding Techniques

Some seeds will germinate in less than a week and others may require several weeks. Most annuals will germinate in about 10 days.

Seed catalogs and seed packages often state the days required, and when the time is close the seeding containers need to be inspected daily for signs of germination and removed to light for growing on.

To help in sowing fine seeds, they may be placed in a clean and dry salt shaker. Also, to help in distributing the seeds, they may be mixed with clean dry sand. Another good idea is to use a piece of folded stiff paper to hold the seeds so that they may be tapped with the index finger to distribute. Also, I often use a plastic or glass tube for dispensing the seed, such as a small test tube or a plastic sleeve such as those in which pencil leads my be packaged.

As to covering or sowing depth, my experience is that germination is best by not covering the seeds any more than twice their diameter, although the information on some seed packets suggests three times the diameter. For sowing vegetables outdoors, more depth may be desired if there is a danger of the soil drying out before there is germination and the seedlings are starting to grow.

Growing seedlings in a greenhouse is a lucky endeavor, which I have only been able to do a couple of times at my daughter Lisa's greenhouse in Asheville, North Carolina. However, I have found that use of florescent lights to be a good substitute, and I have grown thousands of seedlings under such lights. After they get about three inches or so high I like to move them outdoors to cold frames or hot beds depending on the temps. Of course, uncovering of the frames in the morning and covering in the evening is a necessary endeavor.

Seedlings are ready to transplant when they have their first true leaves, not the cotyledons or seed parts. Gently remove the seedlings (called "pricking out") so as to not disturb the roots, using a table knife or similar tool If the seedlings are close together, it may be better to remove in bunches or even as a pot full if the container is small. Then, dip the bunch of seedlings a short time in a pan or bowl of water so that the roots may be gently separated. To make holes in the soil for the seedlings, use a pricking out tool or what is called a dibble, which is a round and pointed wood, plastic or metal tool. A large wood pencil also works well. Keep the seedlings in shade for a few days after transplanting, and then they may be given a weak feeding.

Storage

The writer has found that the best way to store seeds is in pill bottles with tight lids. I also often leave the seeds in their packets and put them in a glass jar with a tight lid and keep it in the refrigerator, not the freezer.

I use a clean glass peanut butter jar, and have germinated delphinium seeds and other perennial seeds kept in the jar for 10 years before seeding.

Plugs

In the last several years, many varieties are available as plugs, in which the grower starts the seedlings in flats of thimble size cups. Quality is controlled by machine sowing of the seeds, and the cost of the plugs is often not much more than the cost of the seeds and expense of material for seeding at home. However, it is often necessary to purchase a whole flat of the same color of seedlings. The little seedlings are transplanted into pots and grown on until time to plant in the garden.

Try Growing From Seed

Some gardeners, even those with very nice gardens, may not have the time or care to get involved with growing from seed. However, to me it can be very satisfying to have nice plants and newer varieties which have been successfully started myself from seed and nurtured to full bloom in the garden.

FAVORED PERENNIALS

Perennials are special friends of the writer. Over more than 50 years of gardening in Indiana, Minnesota and Montana, I have grown about 50 different genera of hardy perennials. I have also gardened for several years in southwest Florida, but that is a different ball game (excuse me, I meant gardening game). Some of my favorite perennials include Achillea, Aconitum, Ajuga, Anthemis, Aquilegias, Arabis, Artemisia, Astilbe, Aubrieta, Bergenia, Browalia, Campanulas, Clematis, Coreopsis, Delphiniums, Dianthus, Dicentra, Dictamus, Digitalis, Echinacea, Flax, Gaillardias, Geum, Heliopsis, Hemerocallis, Heuchera, Hostas, Lavender, Lysimachia, Lupines, Meconopsis, Monarda, Nepeta, Oenothera, Penstemon, Platycodon, Rudbeckias, Salvia, Sedums and Shasta Daises (Leucanthemum).

The following two pages are photos of some perennials grown by the author.

LIST OF PERENNIALS GROWN BY AUTHOR

Achillea
Aconitum
Ajuga
Alstromeria
Anchusa
Anthemis
Aquilegia
Arabis
Artemisia
Aster frikarti
Astilbe
Aubrieta
Bergenia
Browalia
Campanula
Clematis
Coreopsis

Delphinium
Dianthus
Dicentra
Dictamus
Digitalis
Echinacea
Euphorbia
Flax
Gaillardia
Geum
Heliopsis
Hemerocalis
Heuchera
Hostas
Lavender
Leucanthemum
Liatris
Linum

Lunaria
Lupine
Lysimachia
Meconopsis
Monarda
Myosota
Nepeta
Oenothera
Papaver
Penstemon
Platycodon
Physotegia
Rudbeckia
Polemonium
Salvia
Saponaria
Sedums

NEWER PERENNIALS

There is a new group of columbines named Aquilegia Clementine. The plants are compact and short and have upward facing flowers. They prefer well drained soil and attract butterflies. The colors are white, blue, purple, red and rose. Achillea Tutti Ftutti Strawberry is a strong plant with pink flowers, about 24 inches in height and it prefers full sun and well-drained soil. It also attracts butter-flies, along with Asclepias. Hello Yellow is a new color of Asclepias, which do not need fertilizer and prefer sandy soil. Campanula Pink Octopus has bright pink flowers with long drooping petals. The plants grow about 12 to 18 inches and prefer full sun or a little shade.

Coreopsis Sunfire is a golden yellow with a burgandy base and is about 18 inches tall. It blooms in full sun from June to October in the northern states. A new coneflower Echinacea Cheyenne Spirit grows to 20" to 30" high and 20" wide. They bloom in many colors and attract birds and butterflies. Echinacea Pixie Meadowbrite is a beautiful new coneflower, only 16" to 24" high and covered with brilliant darkish pink blossums. It grows in full sun or partial shade. Geranium Alice is a small new plant, only about 8" high with large lilac-pink blossums. It is nice for rock gardens or groundcovers and blooms all summer in full sun.

PERENNIALS OF THE YEAR:

The 2008 Perennial of the Year was a Geranium named Rozanne.
The 2009 Perennial of the Year was Hakonechloa macra "Aureola."
The 2010 Perennial of the Year was Baptisia Australis.
The 2011 Perennial of the Year was Amsonia hubrichtii.
The 2012 Perennial of the Year was Brunnera "Jack Frost."
The 2013 Perennial of the Year was Polygonatum odoratum "Variegatum.
The 2014 Perennial of the Year was Panicum virgatum—switchgrass
Also, some of my gardening friends are particularly fond of hostas, so
I will note the more recent hostas of the year:
2009 Hosta named Earth Angel
2010 Hosta named First Frost
2011 Hosta named Praying Hands
2012 Hosta named Liberty
2013 Hosta named Rainforest Sunrise
2014 Hosta named Abiqua Drinking Gourd

Other interesting perennials include the yellow Ligularia "Twilight" that is 2-3 feet tall and has yellow flowers; a yellow Rudbeckia named "Goldquelle" that does not have a black eye; a dwarf Goldenrod "Little Lemon" that is only 12" tall; and a Tricyrtis Samurai, which is a toad lily with light purple spots.

PERENNIALS IN NORTHERN GARDENS

In earlier years, the writer lived in suburban Minneapolis and had large flower gardens which were toured most weekends during the summer. I retired in 1993, and my wife Wanda and I moved to the Big Sky Ski Resort, about 15 miles north of Yellowstone Park. However, finding that such winters were not good for my arthritis, we soon purchased a home near the beach in Bonita Springs, Florida. We then lived in Montana from mid May to mid October, and the remainder in Florida.

This memo is about gardening in northern parts of the country, and specifically at higher elevations in Montana. Our home there was at about 7000 feet, with a short growing season of about seven weeks. I tried to grow hostas, daylilies, clematis, delphiniums, penstemons and sedums, but I learned that several of my favorite perennials lived a couple of years or so and several did not survive. When we moved to Montana, we took about 75 hostas and daylilies and a few clematis and other perennials, only a few of which survived more than a couple years. We did learn that some perennials, such as delphiniums, survived a few years with a little cover. However, most years there was good snow cover, so we were concerned that use of much straw cover might cause rotting of the plants in the spring. To summarize, the higher elevations in the northern mountains are not the easiest place to grow perennials, but it can be done.

BEAUTIFUL DELPHINIUMS

Delphiniums are one of the most special and beautiful flowers grown in gardens today. The striking and showy delphinium is often called the Queen of the Border. There are varieties from 24 inches to over 6 ft. The taller varieties create a beautiful background presence for flower borders, but require good staking. It is thought that ancient Greeks named the plant delphinium because the unopened buds of the flowers had some resemblance to Dolphins, with a snout more or less elongated into a beak.

I have grown delphiniums in Indiana, Minnesota and Montana, and as annuals in south Florida. Most flowers have been special for me, but delphiniums have always been my favorite.

I first started growing flowers from seed, primary annuals, as a boy living in Indiana. However, most years I only saw those flowering in May, since my father always worked in construction in other states and when I was out of school we would travel to be with him. After getting my engineering and law degrees, in June of 1959 I was hired to practice law in Minneapolis with a patent and trademark firm. I specialized in trademark law and wrote a law book on the subject.

With my wife Anne and first son Louis we bought a home in suburban St. Louis Park, which had quite a lot of space for gardens. I joined the Mens Garden club of Minneapolis, started growing plants from seed and had some nice gardens. Within a couple of years, I was germinating and growing at least 100 delphinium seedlings a year, along with other annuals and perennials.

My experience is that delphiniums germinate well if a few rules are followed. Use a sterile seeding medium, such as good soil, sand and fine peat moss sterilized in the oven. Cover the seeds with about 1/4 inch of milled spaghnum moss or peat moss mixed with sterilized potting soil. After sowing, cover the flat or pot with some glass or plastic for moisture retention and add a magazine or some layers of newspaper to keep the seeding medium totally dark. Keep the seeding pots in a cool place, 60 to 65 degrees F. is best, and look for germination in about 10 days.

As soon as the seedlings begin to appear, place them in a greenhouse or under lights. Prick the seedlings out of the pots when the first true leaves appear. When the seedlngs have gained some strength, I like to take them out to a heated frame or later into a cold frame to grow into nice seedlings for planting out when the weather is right. Seed sown the first few days of February in Minnesota will produce a single bloom spike around the first of August, permitting one to see the color and form. My preference for the garden is to select the shorter plants around 40 inches to five feet since delphiniums of that size are not so difficult to stake. A good true blue is special but rather rare since the florets are often tinted with shades of lavender or purple.

A few cultural tips may be helpful. In the garden, it is suggested that the plants be placed about 3 feet apart in a well prepared soil. Double digging is good, as suggested above under Soil Preparation. Delphiniums have deep roots of at least 12 inches and are heavy feeders. After the first year, thin the shoots to only three. Older plants look nice with five stalks, but ruthless thinning is often required. I have even grown older plants (such as five years) with seven spikes. Do the thinning when the stems emerge 3 to 4 inches by cutting the smaller ones with a knife, making the cuts a couple of inches above the ground. DO NOT pull the stems since this will often cause fungus diseases in the crown and kill the plants. I like to space the surviving shoots rather evenly around the plants to make a nice show when the plants bloom.

Staking is also important. Strong bamboo stakes are placed in a triangle around each plant, and raffia or twine is tied around the stakes about every 12 or 15 inches as the plants grow. I prefer raffia since it is not as visible as twine. Some growers use 1/4" steel rebar rods for stakes since they do not break, but I prefer the appearance of the bamboo. I loop the raffia around one of the stakes to keep it at the elevation desired. Also, do not tie the individual plant stalks to the stakes since we want them to move with the wind inside the "basket" formed by the stakes and twine.

After the main flower stalks have faded, cut just below the bottom florets and then enjoy the lateral shoots, which are nice to use for floral arrangements. After flowering cut the stalks just below the laterals and leave them until autumn clean-up. Should we cut the stems low, it will tend to encourage a second flowering in the autumn, and the plants will not harden off and likely will not survive the winter, at least in the more northern regions. Some growers use a little cover for the winter, but I find that if the stalks are cut about eight inches above the ground, they will catch some leaves from surrounding trees or shrubs and provide enough natural cover.

In the United Kingdom, delphiniums (and some other perennials) are sold as name varieties propagated from cuttings (just like roses), which is nice since plants grown from seed vary from the parents. Taking cuttings can be tricky and is a skill to learn. The problem is that cuttings need a cool place to root with a little sun, and in the U.S. warm weather often arrives rather early. I found cuttings could be rooted in water in glass jars in a window with some sun but not over about 65 degrees F. I have rooted cuttings of about 4 inches, but the cuts must be made where the shoot joins the crown (taking a little of the crown tissue), or they will not root.

The Delphinium Society has some excellent booklets on delphinium culture, including seeding and cuttings. The Society is an international group with several hundred members. It also publishes a Yearbook of some 100 pages with many color photos. The Yearbook is delightful and very useful. Members may purchase delph seeds, and the Society is the best source of seeds. The plants and seeds available in the U.S. are mainly from southern California, and such are not nearly as hardy as those from the U.K. Delphs I have grown from California seed have for me never lasted more than two years at the most in my gardens in Minnesota and Montana. In comparison, my plants from Society seed have often lasted 12 to 15 years in such states.

To join the Society or to purchase seeds, write to David or Shirley Bassett, Cherry Barn, Ells Lane, Broughton, Banbury OX15 5EE, England U.K. Request seed list and info on prices. For membership only, write to Roger Beauchamp, 2 The Grove, Ickenham Uxbridge, Middlesex UB108QH. Membership for 2014 is $25 including postage for Yearbook.

The photos above and on next four pages show delphiniums of numerous colors as grown by the author.

CANNAS

The writer has always liked perennials, but I grow some annuals for color and to fill in between the perennials. I enjoy cannas and they have been a favorite since they are quick growing plants with beautiful foliage and large flowers. Canna leaf colors may be reddish-purple, bronze or green. They are effective for larger gardens, but their size and vigor indicate that they are not so good for restricted areas, particularly for smaller gardens. Cannas like sun, watering and regular fertilization.

Also, they do well with colorful or larger plants like caladium, coco casia (elephant's ear), cratons and castor beans. There are also some newer varieties of elephant's ear which are a beautiful purplish color. Cannas seem to grow best from starts sectioned from older tubers and those having several strong buds. I prefer to plant them about 4 to 5 inches deep, as well as 12 to 18 inches apart.

Canna varieties vary from dwarfs of about two feet to over six feet. The flowers are quite colorful and so is the foliage. The newer varieties with brightly colored leafs are also useful for flower arrangements. Since need to avoid frost, it is good to plant them when doing tomatoes. Like tomatoes, cannas are heavy feeders and thirsty. They also like nitrogen and seem to do well with a 10-10-10—fertilizer.

After the tops have been killed by frost, they should dry a few days and then be cut off. The tubers or rhizomes should be dug and dried in a sunny area for a day or so, and then stored in a cool (50-55 degree F) and moderately dry (30% humidity) cellar or other cool area. I have read that it is best to store the tubers in dry sphagnum moss, vermiculite or sand, in a good place for storing potatoes. It is also a good idea to protect the tubers from insect damage and rot by dusting them with an insect-fungicide powder, such as one part diazinon or sevin to one part fungicide such as captan, maneb or zineb. As for purchasing cannas in the spring, many garden centers carry dormant tubers as well as plants growing in pots. They will often also have canna seeds.

DRYING PLANTS

In late summer, I have thought of trying to dry some of the colorful and beautiful plants from the gardens for use in the home or for gift arrangements. When previously reading articles about drying flowers, I was discouraged by the process of covering plants with moisture absorbent materials, such as Borax. So, some time ago I decided to try the old method used in drying herbs and everlastings, namely merely hanging some of my annuals and perennials upside down in a dry place. One thing I realized was that the larger florets on the plants might tend to drop or shatter, but I thought perhaps that this could be minimized by spraying with a clear lacquer. The results were positive, and after explaining the procedure and results to some of my gardening friends, they also dried some plants.

Since delphinium spikes were my favorite larger plants, and relatively plentiful, I first cut a few dozen spikes and hung them upside down in our lower level or basement. Such space is also air conditioned and quite dry, and I merely hung the spikes over pipes in the furnace and storage room.

Upon cutting the spikes, I of course stripped the leaves, and placed the spikes in layers in a wheelbarrow for transporting through the garage and into the basement area. I tied a length of twine or string to the lower end of a spike, extended the string over the pipe and tied on another spike. By adjusting one spike lower than the other, they were arranged so that they did not get friendly.

In about two or three weeks, the numerous plants were nice and dry, and I did another batch of some other varieties. However, to support the dried delphinium spikes, to prevent damage, and to display for selection in making arrangements, I used a large piece of two inch thick foam board, punching or drilling rows of holes, and inserting the spikes upright. For other plant material, I collected and dried bunches of plants having nice texture or flower heads, such as achillea (yarrow), sedum spectabile, statice, and a nice tall gray sage-like veronica.

After the delphinium spikes were dry, I sprayed them a couple of times with a clear polyurethane from an aerosol container. I would think that spray lacquer, enamel, or ordinary hair spray, would also work nicely. When spraying, I moved the plants into the garage to avoid fumes in the house, after first removing the automobiles o·f course. The spraying worked and prevented the plants from shattering when handled while making arrangements, and also worked as a preservative. With some of the other plant material, such as yarrow and sedum, I sprayed the flower heads a gold or ruby color for a nice contrast with the bluish delphiniums. This time I used an aerosol spray paint, which is available in many colors.

The delphinium colors did fade a little, but still provided nice colors and effect in arrangements. There are few other plants which have the shape, form, color, and appeal of delphinium spikes, fresh or dried. For some of the blue or dirty lavender shades of delphiniums, I sprayed with a nice blue paint to enhance the colors in the arrangements. The result is somewhat artificial to the eye of a discriminating delphinium grower, but one or two bright blue spikes was rather pleasant in the arrangements which I made.

After the plant material was dry and sprayed, as noted, I carried it all into my basement shop area, which was combined with the laundry room. I also collected some other dried plant stems to use as filler material with the delphinium stems. The collection of dried plants, vases, and filling material presented quite a mess for a few weeks, provoking a "few" remarks from my good wife. However, as time permitted, I began making some arrangements which she really liked.

For containers or vases, I had collected quite a few inexpensive glass vases from various sources, as well as some older pottery we did not particularly value. I spray painted the glass vases white, which seemed to look nice with the dried plants. I had enough containers and plant material to make about two dozen arrangements of varying sizes to give away to friends and guests and for casual holiday gifts.

We enjoyed cut flowers in our home, and I often brought in flowers from the garden and made bouquets. I have never been much of a flower arranger, despite having several books on the subject, and admiring the lovely arrangements of delphiniums shown in the Yearbooks of The Delphinium Society. In making my arrangements, I put a little sand in the bottom of the containers for weight, filled them with perlite, and then placed a few delph spikes of varying colors. I then filled in with the other dried plants, trying to balance the shape and colors, and hiding the taller stems with lower material in front.

Most of my arrangements, whenever made, seem to turn out similar in form, what I refer to as a cottage or country bouquet. Anyway, the results were reasonably pleasing, and the gift bouquets were gladly accepted by family, friends and guests. I also recall taking a couple of larger arrangements to our church placement adjacent the altar, and they were much appreciated.

There are many plants which dry nicely. I merely used what was available in our garden to enhance the delphinium spikes, which were the primary objective of my drying and arranging effort. Reference to any good seed catalog will disclose plants and varieties suitable for drying or so called "ever-lastings," many of which should look nice with delphiniums and perhaps not require spraying.

The advantages of spraying with a clear lacquer type coating are to prevent shattering, opening of seed capsules and dropping of seeds or sepals, some preservative action, and some protection against collection of dust. Particularly for the delphiniums or other flowers having large florets or petals, spraying a couple of times with the clear lacquer or polyurethane seems to effectively prevent shattering, which I expected to be the primary problem in drying delphiniums. The process is relatively easy, inexpensive, and provides a nice way to enjoy and share the summer delphiniums for a long time.

ANNUALS FOR QUICK COLOR

There are many nice annuals, most of which germinate easily and are relatively easy to grow. It is also simple to purchase them in packs or flats at garden centers. Obviously, they are called annuals since they thrive and flower for only one summer and then die back (unless of course they are grown in southern Florida). If an individual's garden has mostly weed-free soil and uses mulch, the annuals will require minimal care. After the annuals have bloomed, it is nice to remove the dead flowers and cut back the foliage to avoid a messy appearance and to prevent self-seeding. However, many annuals will flower again if the dead flowers are removed (so-called dead-headed). .

It is easy to sow the seed for annuals every spring, in seed trays, pots or flats or directly in the garden. Also, young plants may be easily purchased in the spring. The following annuals are enjoyed by the writer.

My favorite is the snapdragon, or antirrhinum. They have long lasting flowers in many nice colors, including white, yellow, orange, and violet to a very dark red. They also enjoy sun and a rich but well drained soil. They are available in strains from 10" to 3 feet. Otherwise, I will note alphabetically the annuals I prefer. They are also a very nice cut flower.

Ageratum is a nice plant, normally about 12 to 20 inches, with white, pink, blue or purple colors. They are nice for edgings, window-boxes, rockeries and lower plantings in borders, and prefer a moist but fertile and well drained soil. Watering is necessary in dry weather.

Amaranthus or love-lies-bleeding is a beautiful red or crimson flower about 24 to 30 inches tall, with nice pale green leaves. The plants are pretty in the mid areas of borders, and I have also seen them used in pots. They prefer sun and a moist but rich and well drained soil. These plants are nice as cut flowers and also in dried arrangements.

Calendulas are desireable cut flowers and remind me of asters. However, they have yellow, cream or orange flowers. They prefer moist, medium heavy soil, and grow from about 12" to a little over two feet. Calendulas like to self-seed and send up new plants each year.

Clarkia's silky, papery flowers seem to flower most of the summer. They like fertile well-drained soil, but not real hot weather. They do well in flower beds planted in mass.

Cleome or Spiderflower appears to look rather bizarre. They generally have white flowers (but sometimes pink or violet) with long and protruding stamens that appear to look like spider legs. The plants pre-fer full sun and a somewhat rich but sandy soil. To encourage re-flowering, the seedpods need to be regularly removed.

Coreopsis tinctoria or golden tickseed has reddish flowers with a yellowish pom-pom center, and is a brilliant flower for the garden or pots. They will like any type of well-drained soil in sun or semi-shade. Dead flowers should be removed for repeated blooming.

Cosmos have pink flowers which are luxuriant and rather large, and also have feathery and dainty leaves. The flowers prefer warm, moist but well-drained soil which is also fertile. Removal of the dead flowers extends the flowering season.

California Poppies or Eschscholzia are striking bowl-shaped flowers which appear to have been painted. The 12" plants may be white, pink, yellow, orange or red. I like these flowers in rockeries, the plants have bluish-green pinnate foliage. The flowers tend to open fully only in full sun. A poor but well-drained soil in complete sun is recommended.

Felicia or blue marguerite presents many daisy-like flowers which are sort of a lavender-blue, with dark green foliage. These pretty plants only need sun and a well-drained soil, which may be rather poor. They will not flower much if it rains.

Gazanias, 8 to 12 inch plants, are sometimes referred to as the treasure flower and have flowers in white, yellow, pink, orange and red, and worship the sun. In the shade or when it rains, the flowers will not open. Accordingly, full sun with a sandy and well drained soil is desirable. Removal of the dead flower heads and addition of a little fertilizer will normally extend the flowering time to most of the summer, as long as the temps are moderate.

Gypsoplilia or baby's breath has white or pink flowers, and is particularly nice as a light but bright presence for summer gardens. These bushy plants grow up to 24" and display many impressive star type flowers. They do not need much water or nutrients, but do like lime in the soil and full sun. I stake and tie the taller plants to keep them from bending over.

Helianthus or common sunflower are beautiful and striking flowers that grow to 5 or 6 feet and have yellow-gold or bronze-red flowers up to 6 inches in diameter. They like a good supply of water and nutrients and a well-drained soil. I have planted them in front of fences as a background. There is also a dwarf variety known as "Teddy Bear," which grows up to 2 feet but still has pom-pom type flowers up to 5 inches. They also do well in pots or other containers.

Impatiens. These dwarf bushy plants of 6" to 18" present an abundance of flowers in a wide range of colors including white, pink, orange and deep violet. They like a moist soil with humus and drainage, as well as regular watering and a little periodic fertilizer.

Lavatera "White Beauty." This annual mallow with funnel like flowers is about 24 to 30 inches in height and may be nicely used with perennials. A good well-drained soil is also preferred.

Lobelia. This little 6 inch plant is nice for edging and as a ground cover. It also works well in containers with moist soil including humus, and likes sun or semi-shade. Lobelias germinate well in sun in the spring, but the seeds germinate best if not covered.

Sweet Alyssum. If you like fragrant dwarf plants averaging 3" to 10," this is a good plant for edging or as a ground cover, and also works well between pavers or in cracks in walls. I like it in white and pink, and the spreading flowers nearly cover all the foliage. It prefers sun and a weak or nutrient-poor soil. It is also self-seeding from spring to early autumn.

Matthiola or tenweeks stocks. This is another dwarf plant, nice for edgings and containers. The blooms are early and long lasting. They seem to like any well-drained moist soil.

Nemesia. This white and purple ground cover blooms profusely in summer beds, low pots, dish gardens, flower boxes and other containers. It is usually 8" to 10" and blooms from spring to late summer.

Nicotiana is a relative of tobacco. It is normally about 12" in height and grown as an annual, but may sometimes live a couple of years. The plant is rather bushy in form and tends to bloom most of the day. In a moist, sheltered and well-drained location it will bloom repeatedly, but needs some dead-heading and watering if there is no rain.

Petunia. This common flower is likely the most popular annual. It grows about 10 to 24 inches and comes in many nice colors. The flowers are relatively large and veined, and the plants bloom from spring to the first autumn frost. They do well in containers as well as flower beds or borders. A well-drained soil with some fertility is desired, as is removal of dead flowers.

Phlox drummondii. These classic garden plants are normally about 12 to 18 inches high and come in many nice colors. The attractive plants are rather bushy and do well in most any summer planting. They prefer full sun with a well-drained soil with humus. If cut back to about 6 inches after flowering, a second bloom may likely appear.

Portulaca or moss rose. These plants are sometimes called "everbloomers" and the satiny flowers in rose or dark pink colors like to grow in about any type of soil, but prefer a sandy, dry and hot location. They do not like a lot of water and lower temperatures. These short plants particularly do well as ground covers and in rockeries and containers.

Salvia farinacea or sage grows up to 24 inches, does well in borders or rockeries, also makes a nice front for taller perennials. It is a perennial in areas without frost, but annuals where there is frost. The flower spikes have a silvery soft foliage and the small flowers are a lavender or purplish color. These plants do not demand much care, and they like a dry well drained soil in full sun.

Coleus plants are popular and have nice colorful foliage. They are neat, attractive and easy to grow. The foliage is normally red, dark pink or green, with yellow edges. The leaf edges may be smooth, serrated or wavy. Coleus are easy to start from seed and do well in shade with well drained soil and some humus.

Marigolds. These large pompom blossoms in shades of bright yellow or light orange and dark green foliage grow about 2 to 3 feet . Marigolds are easy to grow and seldom need staking. Being taller, they are excellent as mid-range or backside plantings for flowerbeds or borders, as well larger containers. They are generally sturdy, easy to take care of, and provide a nice balance for other plantings.

Feverfew flowers are 12 to 24 inch plants having very pretty daisy-like white flowers with a yellow center. They are easy to grow and do well in about any soil. The white flowers provide a nice frontage for plants of darker colors. They are short-lived perennials in warmer climates, but are grown as annuals in the north.

Nasturtiums. These bushy dwarf annuals of about 12 inches normally have single flowers. They grow in little mounds with many orange flowers. They will grow in most types of soil, but prefer a poor, moderately dry soil in sunny locations. They can be used in containers and in flower beds and borders, as well window-boxes.

Zinnias. These popular annuals may be of different sizes and shapes and some difference in height. The flowers are somewhat velvety and come in about every color. They will grow in sun or semi-shade, prefer fertile, well-drained soil and are terrific cut flowers which last several days.

VARIETY OF BULBS

To have beautiful blooms in the garden in the spring, autumn is the time to plant bulbs. Most such bulbs are planted only one autumn, and they will bloom year after year in the spring. The rhizomes or corms store the plants energy and will grow the new plants. After the blooms have faded in the spring or early summer, the bulbs may be dug and replanted in a different area if desired.

Tulips and daffodils are the most common bulbs planted by gardeners, but there are several other kinds of bulbs which are nice to grow and increase the time for blooms. Also note that daffodills are now available in white and orange colors. Some of the more unusual bulbs are little in size and are sometimes referred to as minor bulbs. The groups of minor bulbs need more to make a show, but several are fragrant. It is also nice to plant the smaller bulbs in drifts around the lawn, making a bulb meadow.

These three photos show some annuals in author's garden.

Galanthus or Snowdrops are early blooming bulbs for light shade, and they will naturalize to make a spreading display. Crocus are nice flowers in bright colors of white, yellow and light purple. They are welcome blooming in the lawn in early spring. Chinodoxas (sometimes called snowflakes) also bloom early, often coming through the snow, and their small flowers are pale blue with a whitish center. Winter Aconite also blooms early and has yellow flowers that come from tiny bulbs. Scilla is also a small bulb that grows nearly everywhere and is hardy, with true blue flowers. They are also an important early source of nectar. The tiny iris reticulata blooms early and has beautiful purple flowers. Snowflake is about 10" in height and its many sweet little flowers are something like lily of-the-valley. Alliums are of the onion family and their large purple flowers are usually taller (3-1/2 to 4 feet) than surrounding plants and bloom from spring to earl summer. Muscari or grape hyacinths are a common spring plant with clusters of tiny bluish-purple flowers. They are striking when planted en masse. They also do well when planted en masse or in containers with other bulbs. Also important is that deer will not eat them.

In northern areas, it is best to plant bulbs somewhat deeper, such as at least four times the diameter of the bulbs. Also, put a little phosphorous in the planting holes. Most important is to do all the fall planting before the snow comes.

SEMPERVIVUMS

The name sempervivum translates as "live-for-ever." However, many succulents are tender and will not survive the cold in our northern states, although some will. Semps, as they are often called, or succulents, do well in pots, as ground covers, around pavers or steps, in spaces or edgings around stones, and they also provide good drainage. All plants which store water in their stems, leaves or roots are succulents. Aloes, echeverias, hens and chicks, kalanchoes and sedums are all succulents. From the time they come up in the spring, they have many different textures and forms such as fringed, velvety, tufted and smooth. The semps also sometimes seem metallic or opalescent. Further, they have a wide range of colors from silver to bluish, pinkish and purple. Also, some form rosettes and some look like stones. Semps are easy to propagate and they produce multiple chicks each season. In summary, the color, texture and variety of semps is intriguing, and the ease of propagation and low maintenance factors provide years of gardening satisfaction.

I have read that sedums are a nearly perfect plant. For example, the tall "Autumn Joy" provides interest all season. In my opinion, it is hard to find a better all around sedum or a more dramatic sculptural plant. One thing I enjoy is succulents in dish gardens, such as in clay or metal dishes, saucers, bowls or troughs. They are easy to plant and maintain. They also do well in pots. Many of the semps or succulents produce nice flowers, but the writer prefers to select plants based upon the texture and color of the foliage. For planting, I prefer to use 1/3 potting soil, 1/3 sand, and 1/3 perlite. When planting saucers or pots, I like to use a taller plant in the middle such as a kalanchoe, with smaller sedums around the edges. There are many places to use succulents in pots or saucers, but I enjoy them surrounding the edge of a deck, terrace or patio, or the top of a garden wall.

CONTAINER GARDENING

Some gardeners may be limited by their smaller yard space or may not have the time and energy to work the soil and plant a garden. With this in mind, a nice display of plants may be grown in various containers, although it may be noted that space for the plants and energy for growth may be limited. However, by gardening in containers, gardeners may be able to plant a productive, colorful and enjoyable garden.

In choosing a container, one should consider the size of the planter in relation to the desired plants. Smaller pots may be easier to move or to place on raised areas such as tables or benches; whereas larger containers may not be so easy to handle because of their weight, but can be placed on decks or patios. However, also to consider is that water and fertilizer will normally be needed more often in smaller containers, which may require extra effort.

Another thing about containers is that older pots or containers, etc. may have an antique or weathered appearance which may be desired by those who like antique things, but newer bright planters may be more desired by gardeners who prefer contemporary or bright planters. These issues may also be related to the style of a residence and garden.

There are also various issues to consider in choosing the style and characteristics of containers. For example, all containers need ample drainage holes. If there are not any or they are not big enough, new holes should be drilled in relation to the size of the containers. Also, it is suggested that gardeners consider their climate. Metal containers or pots may be left outside during the winter without damage, but clay or even plastic pots may likely crack or break. Also, consider the specific composition of the containers. For example, glass, metal and plastic containers are not porous and hold moisture longer, but are not as natural looking as materials such as clay or wood which may be damaged by winter freezing. Clay pots also loose moisture more quickly in dry weather and require more frequent watering. Containers made of wood, such as planters and window boxes may be sometimes lined with plastic and will therefor be less likely to be damaged by winter freezing. Also, when lined with plastic, the planters should require less watering.

When gardening with containers, a good potting mix should be used. See the chapters above related to Soil Preparation and Starting From Seed (under Medium) for information on recommended potting mixes. It is also simple to purchase potting mixes in about any garden center, hardware store or building center. However, it is much less expensive to mix your own. One thing I do when mixing my own soil is to add a time release fertilizer such as Osmocote. Perlite and vermiculite are also good additives to reduce weight and increase drainage.

When planting containers, here are a few more suggestions. Check to be sure the containers are clean. If the containers are deep or large, some foam peanuts may be added to reduce the required potting mix. When the containers are full of potting mix, plant the flowers or vegetables but be careful as to spacing, with one or more taller plants in the center and smaller plants in the outer areas, and water as normal. On days when it is quite hot, smaller containers may need to be watered more often.

DECK GARDENS

This writing relates to the layout of decorative planters on a deck as an alternative to railings, which the writer believes is more useful and functional. I thought about heading this section with the title "A Railing Not A Railing." Our home in Montana has a rather large front entry deck adjacent large windows with views of the mountains and our gardens. The drop off to the ground is only 18 inches, and when we built we were told that building codes did not require a railing if the drop to the ground is not more than 18 inches. However, we entertained quite a lot and were concerned that even an 18 inch fall off an open deck was not very safe, particularly for elderly people.

These photos show some plant containers made by the author.

We were also concerned that railings on the decks would hinder our views, since the code required that railings be at least 40 inches high and pickets not more than five inches apart. I therefore came up with this design for our front entry, which is useful and decorative. It also provides a safe barrier to prevent someone from falling off the deck, and further provides extra seating which may be needed when hosting larger groups. It is emphasized that where we built these planter-seats, no railing or barrier was legally required but we built planter-seats as an extra precaution. Codes in your area may differ and the writer makes no representation about this design complying with any building codes anywhere.

The basic idea is to have some easily maintained planter boxes, alternately spaced and tied together with seating. This design, in my view, is rather contemporary and sturdy looking, but still functional. I think the proportions are attractive, but admit that I was also concerned with using left over lumber. I had a supply of left over 2" x 6" Douglas fir lumber and some 5/4 decking. Also, I wanted planters wherein a special liner did not have to be made nor the soil removed in the winter, and removal or protection of the planting container was not a big problem.

The accompanying photos show the general design. The boxes are built to accept a standard 5 gallon plastic bucket as the planter. Placing pieces of 2" x 10" (really 1-1/2" x 9-1/2') wood in the bottom makes the buckets top out at nearly the top of the wood boxes, which are made by using the 2" x 6" lumber. Should one wish to secure the planters to the deck, it could easily be done with screws. Also, I seldom removed the buckets of soil in the winter, but merely placed pieces of exterior plywood on top of the buckets to exclude moisture and prevent freezing damage to the buckets. With the dry autumn climate in Montana, the buckets of soil had little moisture by the time I wished to cover them for the winter.

Before planting the buckets in the spring, I drilled a few 1/4" holes in the bottom of the buckets for drainage, put in an inch or so of gravel, and then three inverted 4" or 5" plastic pots to save soil and reduce weight. My recollection is that I also used some styrofoam pellets. We filled the buckets with a nice soil mix, and in most pots planted just one seedling of Wave petunias. The planters were soon covered with the spreading plants which would grow to about three feet during our short seven week mostly frost-free growing season. The rectangular planters are made of inside and outside layers of 2" x 6" lumber, screwed together with galvanized screws.

One-eighth inch pilot holes were drilled in the lumber to prevent splintering of the wood. The reason for two layers of wood for the boxes was that the outer layer was 1-1/2" lower to make a 1-1/2" space to support the seats placed between the flower boxes.

The seats were made out of 5/4 western cypress deck lumber, using 3 boards 5-1/2" wide. The ends of the seat boards are screwed to the top of the outer box of the planters. It is preferable to have the seat boards a little shorter than 48" in length to prevent bowing in the middle when people are seating on them. To hold the seating boards together I used some pieces of 1/2 inch exterior plywood screwed to the bottom of the seat boards. To make such a deck seating, the length of the deck is measured, and the number and size of the planter boxes is deducted to determine the length and number of the seats in between the boxes.

The following photos show the deck planters and seats noted above, as well as the elliptical steps noted below.

DECORATIVE STEPS

Another feature of the deck area leading to the main entrance to the home is the pretty elliptical concrete steps designed and made by the writer. The accompanying photos show the flower boxes and seats, as well as a portion of the concrete steps, only two of which were required. The steps are basically elliptical. However, since they fit in a corner of the deck, the right ends have the elliptical configuration, and the left ends are square to fit the corner.

The steps are 24" wide and 72" long by 3" thick. To make the form for the steps, I used a piece of 5/8"plywood for the base and 1/4" strips of Masonite for the edging. The edging or side strips were secured to the base by triangular braces of 2x4 wood screwed to the sheet of base plywood. The screws were inserted from the bottom of the base plywood into the 2x4 braces. Such braces had a 90 degree corner to make the edging strips completely vertical, one side 3-1/2" long to meet the side strips, and the other side about 4" for fastening to the plywood base by screws.

The way to design an ellipse is illustrated in most larger dictionaries. I designed this ellipse by first measuring the exact length and width of the design and laying out such dimensions on a flat surface such as a sheet of plywood or sheetrock. Our design is 72" wide by 24" high. A 72" long line is drawn horizontally and a 24" long line drawn vertically at the exact middle of the long line, making sure it extends 12" up and 12" down at 90 degrees from the horizontal line. Then, take a 72" long and non-stretchable line and put the exact middle of such line at the top end of the 12" vertical line, and where the opposite ends meet the horizontal line, mark such points as foci A and B. By taking the 72" non-stretchable line or a soft bendable wire 72" long, and securing each of the ends at the foci A and B, and then moving the middle of such line or wire around he perimeter, the configuration of the ellipse will be defined. It helps to drive a small nail at each of the foci A and B, and also make small loops in both ends of the wire to place over the nails, whereby it is easier to scribe the perimeter of the ellipse.

Anyway, when the form of the steps was made, I mixed the concrete using an aggregate of mixed washed rock from 1/4" to 3/4", plus sand and portland cement. I used the normal mix of 1/3 aggregate, 1/3 sand and 1/3 cement. After filling the form with the concrete mix and screeding the top to provide a flat surface, I let the concrete set for a while to be firm but still wet enough to permit washing the surface to lightly expose the aggregate. A smooth finished concrete surface may be used, but I prefer some exposed aggregate to make a prettier surface, in my opinion.

After the concrete dried for 24 hours or so, I removed the form from the first step. I then put the form back together and poured the concrete for the second step, being identical. I then made a wood base for the first step out of 2"x4" lumber (3-1/2"), which made the step 6-1/2" above grade, which I believed to be a safe height for a step. Next, I made a wood base for the second step, measuring 10" in height, for a total of 13" above grade. This worked to have each step 6-1/2" high and the same height from the top step to the deck. Guests often remarked about the unique design and nice appearance of the steps.

BUILDING BRICK TERRACES

Depending on the style of home and garden, terraces or patios and walkways made from paving bricks may present an elegant and interesting addition to the landscape. Paving bricks come in different textures and numerous colors. Those used for driveways are about 3-1/2" thick, while those manufactured for walkways, terraces or patios are about 1-1/4" thick (nominally 4"x8"x1").

In more southern climates, bricks (or stone, slate, etc.) may be satisfactorily laid over a tamped bed of sand. However, in northern climes with freezing and thawing, paving materials laid merely over sand will after a couple of seasons have an uneven surface because of frost. To solve this problem, builders will sometimes pour a 4 inch concrete slab as a base and lay the bricks or pavers on top of the stable slab. This is expensive, hard work and difficult for one worker to do alone. Also, if using ready-mix, the driver will not want to wait around while one person handles the job.

Since we wanted to install several brick terraces and walkways at our former home in Golden Valley, Minnesota, I devised a plan to use treated lumber as a base for the paving brick, rather than concrete. The advantage is that one person may handle and install the lumber, and it may be done as time permits. If the worker needs to take a break in the middle of a section, it is not a problem to later start again.

While working on this project, I learned some things which is not unusual. The area to be paved should be well drained, covered with about 4 inches of tamped sand or fine gravel and screeded level. The perimeter is held in place with treated 6"x6" landscape timbers and a flat base of treated 2"x6" boards is screwed to stringers laid crossways underneath about every two feet. If a curved edge is desired, it may be made by two side-by-side 1"x6" boards screwed into the 2"x6" platform. All lumber should be screwed together with brass or stainless screws. My recollection is that the cost of materials (without labor) for this installation is about the same as the cost of concrete, but the labor is much easier for a worker to do alone. The type of lumber obtained for the job should be the kind treated for contact with soil, such as the green treated lumber. The following photos show the brick terraces at the front entry to the author's home in Golden Valley, Minnesota.

When placing the bricks after the wood platform is built, a pattern needs to be selected. Some ideas are shown in the accompanying sketches. A wet saw will need to be rented to make cuts when required. The workmen also need to look carefully at the bricks while laying them. Since such bricks are a natural product, they normally have a slump resulting from the manufacturing process. That is, there is a slight curvature when viewed from the top as well as the side (see drawing). The point is to make sure to lay then all the same way, with the slight curves in the same direction. If this is not done, the lines will soon no longer be straight. When the bricks are all laid, the cracks are filled with a sweeping of fine sand which also stabilizes the paving. The accompanying sketches illustrate the ideas and suggestions explained above.

BRICK TERRACE DETAILS

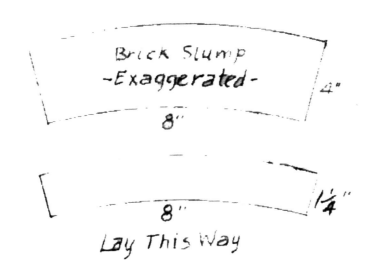

Brick Slump
-Exaggerated-

4"

8"

1¼"

8"

Lay This Way

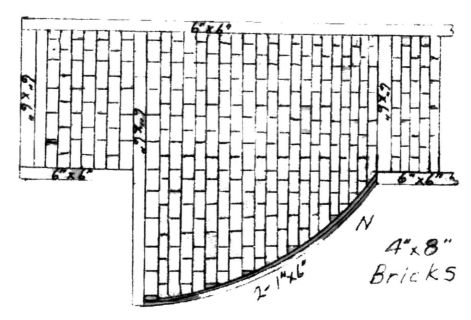

6"x6"

6"x6"

6"x6"

6"x6"

6"x6"

N

4"x8"
Bricks

2-1"x6"

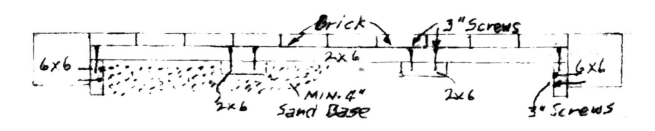

Brick

3" Screws

6x6

2x6

2x6

MIN. 4"
Sand Base

2x6

6x6

3" Screws

GARDEN SCULPTURES

The writer has always enjoyed making things such as furniture, various artwork such as wood, steel and stone sculptures, oil paintings and construction features for my gardens (the decorative elliptical steps noted above could be an example). The photos included below are examples of different types of artwork and gardens all designed, created or built by the author.

The following are photos of the author's garden and garden structures in Golden Valley, Minnesota. The photos listed as 5 through 14 are shown on the following pages.

1. A pergola and steps to one of the back gardens. (Bottom photo p. 3)
2. Arcuate and elliptical steps and a large deck. (Photos on p. 39)
3. Steps, brick terraces and landscaping at front entrance. (Photos p. 42)
4. Stone terraces at end of back gardens. (Photo at bottom of p. 4)
5. A shade garden and Japanese stone lantern made by the author.
6. A "snake" made of flower pots and used as a garden sculpture.
7. A sculpture of wood rings designed to alternately rotate in the wind.
8. A caterpillar sculpture for the garden or indoors.
9. A 30" wide butterfly sculpture cut from 3/32" steel for the garden. see page 46
10. An elephant garden sculpture made of old musical instruments. see page 46
11. A deck chair made of willow branches. see page 47
12. A Canadian goose sculpture carved with a chain saw and painted. see page 47
13. A 6' long fish sculpture made from stainless steel for a deck wall. see page 47
14. A loon sculpture carved from an oak log and painted. see page 47

KOOPMANS GARDEN

Following is a special photo of a large potted plant sculpture designed, made and planted by my friend Roger Koopmans in Faribault, Minnesota. The photo was not taken by the author, but was given to me by the Koopmans. The garden of Roger and Kathleen Koopmans is on a city (continued on page 48)

No. 5

No. 6

No. 7

No. 8

No. 9

No. 10

No. 11

No. 12

No. 13

No. 14

lot and not huge, but I believe it to be one of the most beautiful gardens I have seen anywhere in the U.S. or Europe. They are both great gardeners, grow large variety of annuals and perennials, have several unique and beautiful garden features and sculptures, plus a vegetable garden which everyone cherishes. I have visited their garden many times over the last 50 years and have never seen a weed. See page 50.

JAPANESE STYLE GARDENS

Over the years, I have designed and completed a couple of Japanese style gardens. They have not been extensive, but were enjoyable for me and gardening friends. One such garden was located near our front entry at our first home in St. Louis Park, and the other was located adjacent my front terraced gardens at our home in Golden Valley, both being suburbs of Minneapolis, Minnesota.

The front entry garden in St. Louis Park had a ground cover of smaller flat and smooth rocks collected from the shores of Lake Superior in northern Minnesota. Most of the plants were shorter annuals and perennials. I cannot remember them all, but there were some Japanese anemones, along with a carpet of pachysandra plants about 8 inches and which form a carpet of glossy dark green leaves which are bright at the tips. Also, there was some Virginia creeper, Parthenocissus quinquefolia, which have long leaves that are green in the spring and later turn to a beautiful crimson red. Also, a pretty Japanese stone lantern about 24" in height was designed and created by me from a whitish stone, along with a small stone bowl. I thought that the stone sculptures emphasized the Japanese nature of such garden. The top photos on the following page show the sculptures.

The terraced gardens in Golden Valley had 10" to 16" smooth flat rocks laid on the soil, but with open spaces for plants. The. plants included Lily-of-the-valley about 8" high, some Wild ginger which grows only about 4" high but with beautiful 4" leaves; Vinca minor or periwinkle which is about 8" and has beautiful blue flowers, and some Stonecrop which is a mat-forming succulent which has whitish flowers and is a nice creeper. In the backyard is a small Japanese style garden with a small pool and another taller Japanese lantern designed and created from stone by the writer. See the bottom photo on the following page.

Unique planters at Koopmans garden in Faribault, Mn

One of the gardens at Koopmans

WALL GARDENS

Wall gardens are sometimes built because of property configurations or for steep slopes. However, they may often be desired by gardeners or proposed by landscape architects. In the writer's opinion, walls over about three feet are not very attractive. Further, if a higher wall is desired, it is better to have two shorter wall terraces, which will provide greater stability. In northern climates, deeper foundations below the soil may be required for support and to prevent frost damage to the construction, and drainage or weeping holes are also necessary. Also, the layers of rocks should be mostly level for stability.

Basic wall gardens may be constructed without masonry or cement. The walls are built to hold plants which also help hold the walls. Plants often survive quite well in these walls without masonry. Larger rocks are preferred and rocks with round surfaces should be thrown away since they will not hold anything. Larger rocks extending backward beyond the wall are helpful to keep the wall in place.

Walls for gardens may be constructed from concrete, masonry such as stone or bricks, various types of wood construction such as 4"x4" or larger beams, wood posts, railroad ties, wood planks supported by posts, flat concrete or stone slabs, or various combinations. Lannon stone makes beautiful walls, but can be rather expensive.

If the walls are of much height, such as over 12 inches, they need to be sloped backwards at least 10 degrees or about 2 inches per foot of height. This is to keep the walls tilting backward when frost expands the soil. Also, the tilting backwards keeps the rocks tilting somewhat downwards toward the back to keep the soil from drifting forward and to also direct the flow of rainwater into the wall. With walls made of flat stones or pieces of concrete, the spaces between the layers and joints need to be filled with a soil having some sand. This is to provide drainage and decrease pressure behind the walls. The width of the rocks at the bottom of the wall should be approximately equal to one-third the height of the wall. Bricks and stones can be cut with a masonry saw blade, or trimmed with a cold chisel and heavy hammer. Gloves and safety goggles should be used.

Sitting benches made from 1x4 or 1x6 lumber are attractive, particularly if there is a desire for curves, such as around an oblong or rounded patio or terrace. Care in fastening the slats to periodic spacers is required.

Timber walls can be quite pretty, but do not last as long as stone or concrete. Cedar and redwood are resistant to decay, but will be more resistant to decay if pressure treated. Used railroad ties are sometimes available and perhaps merely for the cost of hauling. I have built several retaining walls with used ties. Even though they are heavy, I nailed them together with 12" x 1/2" nails.

When filling wall gardens with soil, I like to put a few inches of gravel in the bottom, followed by perhaps 4 inches of sand and then some good soil as discussed earlier. Planting the wall gardens with your favorite annuals and perennials will be similar to planting smaller borders, although I prefer to have a nice edging of a creeping type plant, such as creeping phlox, rock soapwort, or sempervivums.

SINGLE COLOR GARDENS

In designing a flower garden, I have normally paid more attention to size and appearance of the plants, believing that colors will pretty much take care of themselves as long as some white plants are included here and there. Any gardener may plant a single color garden, which can be worthwhile and enjoyable if their color is important to them. I had a blue garden quite a few years ago, which had several different blue or bluish varieties. Visitors thought it was special and often talked about it. I considered planting an all red garden but didn't do it.

An all white garden has also been of interest to the writer, but I never found a good place for it. I did include a smaller white section in my main flower border. The effect was pleasing, but my space being limited, I decided after a couple of years to return to a mixed planting. However, I will always remember the all white garden at Sissinghurst in England. See the mention of such estate in the above section Designing Flower Borders.

In the past I have planted some spring bulb gardens of a single color, such as red tulips, all yellow tulips or pink tulips. Of course, all yellow daffodils are nice as are yellow or bluish crocus. Apart from bulbs, gardeners certainly may consider other plants of single colors. For example, Ageratum varieties have a nice purple color, Amaranthus a bright red, Brachyscome a pretty violet, Calendulas a bright orange, cornflowers a nice blue, Coreopsis a brilliant scarlet, Delphiniums a bright blue, Gypsophila or baby's breath a showy white, Marigolds a nice bright yellow, the common sunflower a yellow-gold, petunias come in several bright colors, Rudbeckias have yellow flowers, and Zinnias come in bright orange or yellow flowers.

The problem for me in planting a single color flower garden has been finding the space, or not wanting to dig up one garden to get such space for a specific color. It seems that most gardeners have a hard time finding the space to plant all the varieties they cherish.

SOFTWOOD PROPAGATION

There are two customary ways to easily increase the stock of plants for the garden. One is sexual, that is by seeds, and the other is asexual, or vegetative propagation. Asexual propagation may be accomplished by various means, including stem cuttings, root cuttings, leaf cuttings, stem and air layering, divisions and meristem culture.

For the home gardener, favorite plants may be reproduced and multiplied rather easily by means of stem cuttings. Some years ago, I remember that my friend and Golden Valley neighbor Dave Johnson and I would start impatiens from seed a little earlier than normal seeding time. When the seedlings were a few inches high we would cut off the top couple of inches and root them, thus doubling our stock of seedlings at very little expense.

Some varieties of plants, including both annuals and perennials, root easier than others, and softwood cuttings are generally much easier to root than hardwood cuttings.

Cleanliness is one prerequisite, and care in using sterile materials will increase the success rate. This includes sterilized containers, rooting medium, and the use of alcohol to clean a knife or pruner in between the taking of cuttings. In taking cuttings, some growers recommend the use of a hormone rooting powder, but I have found the same to be unnecessary for the plants I have wanted to reproduce.

Over the years, I have rooted annuals such as coleus, impatiens, begonias and geraniums/pelargoniums. I have also rooted perennials such as dianthus, mums, sedums, delphiniums, geraniums, aubrieta, cerastium, nepeta and saponaria, as well as various house plants.

My usual technique is rather straightforward. The cutting is made just below a leaf node, the lower leaves removed, and the cuttings placed in a cool and shady place for 30 minutes or so to form a callus over the cut surface. The cuttings are then "stuck" into the moist rooting medium. It is best to insert the cuttings so that they are not touching, in order to discourage fungus or rotting of the leaves. The containers of cuttings are placed in a cool but light location out of direct sun. Also, care must be taken to keep the medium moist enough to encourage formation of roots but not so wet as to encourage fungus and diseases. Temperatures below 65 degrees F. also seem to help.

Various materials may be used to support the cuttings in the containers, such as peat moss, vermiculite, perlite, sterile sand or sterile soil. I normally use a mixture of fine vermiculite, perlite, sterile sand or sterile soil. Some growers are successful merely placing the cuttings in water, but for me this often produces brittle and fragile roots. I have however often rooted coleus cuttings in water. Species which root easily, such as mums, can be rooted in moist sand. No matter what the medium, when roots of about half an inch have formed, the plants may be potted up for growing on in the usual manner.

Propagation of special plants by cuttings is an enjoyable and rewarding means of reproducing our favorite plants, either for the garden or for house plants.

STAKING AND TYING

Many plants benefit from some type of support, such as stakes, cages, wire hoops, trellises, etc. In my view, staking and tying is one of the more desirable endeavors supporting appearance of a garden. Staking is a good solution for appearance, but it is seldom completely satisfactory in all weather conditions. There are two primary reasons for staking, to provide support for weaker plants and to help protect taller plants from being bent or broken during storms or high winds.

No matter what type of support is utilized, it should be arranged as much as possible so that the natural beauty of the plants is preserved and the support is not so visible. The accompanying sketches illustrate various techniques found to be effective for flower plants. Vegetables generally need stronger support.

Smaller plants generally need little support. However, some shorter plants which sprawl quite a bit can use some short stakes and a loop of twine to keep the plants in more of a bunch. Sometimes, a short ring of chicken wire placed around the shorter plants will help reduce sprawling.

Mid range perennials, such as pyrethrum, platycodon, veronica, physotegia, etc., and annuals such as the taller snapdragons, petunias, carnations and asters, do well with a three stake arrangement using a couple of ties around the stakes. This is similar to the illustration for delphiniums, but using much shorter stakes. It is good to make a loop around at least one of the stakes with the tying material so that it will stay in place. As to the type of material, it should be soft so as to not bruise the plant stems. My preference is raffia since it has low visibility, but other choices include plastic tape and good twine. Some gardeners I know use cut strips of old panty hose, but I seldom wear them. For mid height plants, trimmings from a twiggy tree or shrub branches make a good staking material. Trimmings from birch or aspen or similar trees are particularly nice for this purpose. While the plants are still small, the twigs are merely stuck in the soil aroundthe plants, and as the plants grow the twigs become invisible. This system is often utilized by gardeners in England. The only disadvantage is the rather unsightly appearance until the twigs are covered by the plant growth.

The taller perennials, such as delphiniums, foxglove and dahlias require taller and stronger stakes. Strong bamboo stakes work well, as do the green plastic coated steel stakes now available (but expensive). I tried using a few of the the steel stakes in Minnesota, but went back to the preferable bamboo.

Plants having primarily only one stalk or stem, such as dahlias, may be successfully supported with only one sturdy stake, using a tie about every 12 inches. However, those plants producing several stems, such as delphiniums, are better supported using three stakes spaced in a triangle about the plants, again with ties placed about every 12 inches as the plants grow. Take care to make a loop of the tie around at least one of the stakes so that the tying stays in place. Delphiniums have stiff hollow stalks and I do not like to tie each stalk to a stake. Unless ties are made quite close together (which I believe is unsightly), the stalks are likely to break in a storm or heavy rain since the flower spikes are quite heavy. I prefer to make ties around the stakes about every 12" to form sort of a "basket" in which the spikes may sway and move in the wind.

Another popular type of support is the metal hoops available commercially. These work well for some plants, such as peonies and phlox or other plants having several blooming stems. Another type hoop sometimes available has a criss-cross of wires in the middle of the hoop, up through which the plant stems may grow.

There are some annuals which have sort of a sprawling or floppy growth, such as some varieties of petunias. For these a small cage made from chicken wire works well to elevate the plant and add some height near the front of the border. A cage about 12-15 inches high and about 12 inches in diameter works well. The idea is to plant three plants of the same color in a small triangle, place the cage over the plants, and pin it to the ground with a couple of stakes woven through opposite sides of the cage. The plants will grow up and through the wire which will become invisible.

An idea similar to the above may be used for a large cage or pillar for the back of the border. Take a piece of wire fencing having spaces about 2" by 4", the fencing being about 5 feet or so in height and about 6 feet long. Bend the fencing to form a column and tie the vertical ends with the cut wire ends or other pieces of wire. After being placed in the desired location, place a couple of steel fence posts on opposite sides and wire the column to the posts. About three clematis plants made be spaced around the exterior of the column, and they will soon cover the fencing. Some care is required to train or guide the young stems so as to fill in spaces and create a solid cover. Annual vines, such as morning glory or cobaea, may also be used. One could also try the perennial trumpet vine Campsis radicans. I have never found it very hardy in Minnesota but it could do well in more southern areas.

It is best for staking and tying to be done on a weekly basis or at least bi-weekly, during the main growing season. It may seem like an onerous chore, but can add significantly to the appearance of the flower border.

ANNUALS PLANTED INSIDE CAGE

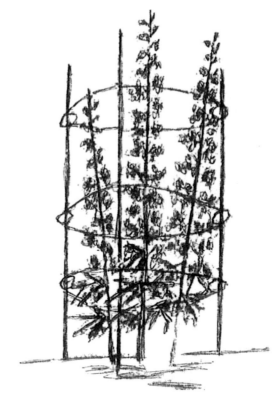

DELPHINIUMS IN A "CAGE OF 3 STAKES WITH TIES AROUND THE STAKES

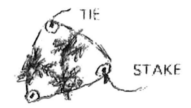

STALKING SMALLER PLANTS

TREE BRANCHES FOR SUPPORT

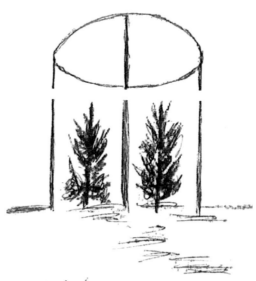

P.H. SMITH

PEONI HOOPS

SHADE GARDENS

Some plants prefer shade or at least partial shade, and if gardeners wish to grow such plants they need to select only a location having adequate shade. Any attempt to grow shade plants in the sun will result in sunburn to the plants and withering of the foliage. Plants in a shade garden may be annuals or perennials. The writer has grown numerous shade plants, but I would not try plants in shade if they are known to prefer sun.

Listed below are varieties I have grown in the shade in Minnesota or Montana, and/or seen growing in the shade at the Minnesota Landscape Arboretum.

Alchemilla mollis—Lady's Mantle
Anemone
Aquilegia—Columbine
Astilbe
Begonia—Tuberous
Begonia—semperflorens (wax)
Campanula carpatica
Campanula glomerata
Campanula lactiflora
Campanula persicifolia
Centaurea—Coneflower
Coleus—mint herb
Dicentra—Bleeding
Heart Dictamnus—Gas Plant
Dodecatheon—Shooting Star
Echinacea purpurea—Coneflower
Feverfew
Filipendula rubra
Forget-me-not
Gentian
Geranium Johnson's Blue

Hemerocallis—Daylilly
Heuchera
Hostas
Impatiens
Leucanthemum—Shasta Daisy
Lobelia
Lunaria
Lupine
Lythrum—purple loosestrife
Marsh Marigolds
Michaelmas Daisy
Monarda—Beebalm
Monkshood
Nicotiana—Tobacco plant
Pansies
Penstemon—Beards tongue
Physostegia—Obedient Plant
Platycodon—Balloon Flower
Pulmonaria—Blue lungwort
Rudbeckia Goldsturm—Coneflower
Trillium

WATERFALLS

The movement and sensitivity of waterfalls has attracted me over the years and I decided to work on building one. I collected some ideas and information, and proceeded to design and build a couple of small waterfall pool areas at my previous properties. However, I began researching ideas and methods new to me, with the plan of constructing a rather large waterfall-pool area at my property located at the resort at Big Sky, Montana.

Waterfalls are becoming more popular landscape features. People are attracted to the serene and peaceful scene generated by water dancing over the rocks in a pretty falls. Rocks seem to be everywhere in Montana, but it takes some talent to arrange and assemble stones into a natural looking falls and stream enhanced with some hardy plants. Aside from the beauty and peaceful features of a falls, another significant attraction is the musical sounds generated by moving water, which may be similar to nature's own streams and falls found in mountain areas.

Where I planned our falls, there is a nice slope about 60 feet in length, an elevation drop of 10 to 12 feet, and a natural base of out cropping rocks. Also, close to the house is a quarry area of about two acres with abundant rocks and boulders of all sizes and shapes. My first effort was to collect many large flat rocks for use in making the edges of the various falls and cantilevered sections. I had a large Bobcat skid-steer loader and a dump truck to use in collecting and moving rocks to the falls location.

The first project is to excavate the various pool or pond areas which will hold some of the water. These areas are bedded with sand and fines from processed gravel, then covered with a thick carpet type material as a cushion, and then a heavy plastic liner to prevent seepage or loss of water into the ground. I used a heavy polyethylene type of material about 1/16 inch in thickness (can't recall the mills) which is made for lining sewage and landscape ponds.

Photos of waterfalls built by author at Big Sky, Montana home.

A fairly large pump is placed in the lowest pool to recirculate the water through 2 inch piping to the highest parts of the falls. Once the project is built and the pools filled with water, only enough water needs to be added periodically to compensate for evaporation and splashing of the falls. The bottom of the pools are covered with flat rocks or stones approximately 2 inches thick to protect the plastic liners from being damaged, such as by deer wading in the pools. It is not recommended that cement or mortar be used to fit the rocks, but that the rocks be sized and fitted together over the heavy liner, as much as possible. Where desired, the rocks are fitted and held together by using the aerosol foam spray used for filling cracks and insulating buildings.

Any pool needs a pump to recirculate the water. Pumps are rated by gallons per minute, and a small pool would need 6 to 10 gpm. I used a fairly large pump with a 2-1/2 h.p. motor and 2 inch pipe fittings. The pump will be a smaller part of the total cost and I recommend a quality brand. Of course, the pump needs to be removed and stored inside for the winter, and the water lines in the falls need to be drained.

In building a larger falls, heavy equipment is necessary to move the larger rocks. A back hoe with a thumb on the bucket can normally lift and place half ton rocks at close range and perhaps 500 pound rocks with the boom extended.

Even a small waterfall will add significant pleasure for a homeowner's patio or deck area, often at moderate expense. If attractive rocks may be acquired locally, the cost of purchasing and transporting materials may be reduced. A waterfall or pool installation can be very pleasing to the eye and ear, but a natural appearance is desired. If you are not skilled in design and construction of this type, use of an experienced company or landscape contractor is recommended.

MORE NICE PLANTS

There are some more nice plants which have added enjoyment to my gardens. These are penstemons, monardas, and dianthus. They have nice colors, some tolerance from drought and disease, nice stature and a desireable blooming time.

PENSTEMONS. The penstemon or beard-tongue is considered hardy to zone 3, at least for many of the more than 250 species, nearly all of which are native to North America. Penstemons in the wild grow on both sides of the Rocky Mountains, some into Canada and many in the southwest. Penstemons are quite pretty and have rather intense colors. They may be a ruby red, bright pink, shades of purple, a clear blue and the standard white. Their flowers are shaped like bells.

The species Penstemon digitalis is native to Arkansas, and is an upright perennial some 40 inches in height that blooms in midsummer and loves sun. There are also some very pretty red varieties, such as 'Rich Ruby' and 'Husker Red', the Perennial Plant Association's perennial of the year in 1996. The variety 'Prairie Dusk' is a beautiful dark pink which seems to glow in the evening light. All penstemons seem to look best in the garden when planted in groups of three of the same color. They also appreciate a relatively dry soil in the summer. Penstemons tend to produce great amounts of seeds and it is best to soon deadhead the blooms after flowering. They look nice with yarrows and day-lilies.

MONARDAS. Of the 19 monarda species, only M. didyma and M. fistulosa are grown by most gardeners and which together include nearly 100 cultivars. Monardas are members of the mint family and have fragrant flowers. They also have several common names such as beebalm, wild bergamot, Oswego tea and horsemint. All of the 19 species are indigenous to North America.

Most monardas flower continuously from early summer to autumn. M. didyma produces an abundance of summer flowers in pink, purple and scarlet. M. fistulosa blooms later with purple and pink flowers. Also, these two species have produced quite a few beautiful hybrids. Other species often grown are M. fruticulosa and M. punctata. The later has been used to relieve fever and stomach ailments, M. fistulosa to remedy colds and flavor meats, and M. didyma to make tea.

Most northerly Monarda species are prarie natives which grow in many states. They are perennial, hardy and often naturalize. Monarda punctata is commonly known as horsemint and grows as far north as zone 4. Most horsemints have yellow flowers, and tend to survive 3 to 4 years in zone 4. M. punctata is a heavy bloomer, likes sandy soils, and the white and yellow colors look quite nice in flower borders.

DIANTHUS. This is a large genus of annual, biennial and perennial plants. They include the pinks, carnations, and various species. Varieties of Dianthus are valuable for their appearance in flower gardens, as well as for their fragrance. The genus is native almost entirely to Europe, with the greatest number of varieties coming from the Balkan Peninsula and Asia Minor.

Dianthus having been grown in Europe for centuries. They were nicknamed pinks, not because of color, but for the uneven, crimped or "pinked" edges of the petals in the blossoms. Another source says that the name pinks was used first in the 1500s as an old English word meaning 'an eye'.

I have grown pinks in my rock gardens in Minnesota and Montana, and have also used them as edging plants and in dry walls. The main color scheme of pinks is red, varying from the deepest or intense crimson to the palest pink. Occasionally there are some white forms as well as lavender.

Pinks seem to enjoy growing about anywhere. They will even tolerate some afternoon sun if they have good moisture. All sedums are shallow rooted, having roots of about 4 inches. It is therefore good for the plants to have a decent mulch, as well a light soil. I prefer to add some leaf mold to the soil for pinks, but certainly no clay.

Dianthus normally need little fertilizer. But, if the plants seem to need some, use a mix high in phosphorous and potassium. This promotes better flowering and more compact foliage. Also, try to get rid of any rabbits in your area, since pinks are one of their favorite foods. I have read of the recommendation to spray the plants with a mixture of a little Epsom salts and water. Also, note the comments below in the Deer Control section, which includes some control of rabbits.

Most pinks bloom in the spring just after the early spring bulbs.

Further, dianthus hybrids will continue to flower after the species have finished if they are not permitted to set seed.

IDEAS FROM GRANDMOTHER

When I was a lad, I enjoyed visits to the farm of my Grandmother Smith, particularly in the summer to see her large vegetable and flower gardens. Her name was Elizabeth but sometimes she was called "Liz." When we visited I even got to help her weed or hoe, once in a while. She was quite a gardener and I expect that may be where my interest in plants was initially encouraged. In remembering her, I find that I still occasionally use some of her ideas and techniques. Some may think they are old fashioned ideas. Well, they are. My grandmother gardened into her eighties and I am now gardening in my seventies. I guess that would qualify as "old."

ROSE JARS FOR CUTTINGS

In the earlier days, many people successfully rooted cuttings of roses and other woody plants by using nothing but an old glass jar, such as quart canning jar. They were normally called rose jars in those days. My grandmother would just cut off a rose stem, stick it a few inches in decent soil in a somewhat shady place, and cover it with a glass jar turned upside down. Placing the cutting between taller plants in a flower or vegetable garden provided some shade, and the jar functioned as a little greenhouse. I have tried it with about a 50°/o success rate. The advantage is that no special equipment is needed and the cutting or cuttings may be taken and stuck whenever the desire arises (except winter of course). Most people known to me no longer have canning jars, but a quart mayonnaise jar works quite well. See Page 65.

WILLOW TEA

The success rate for most any cuttings is enhanced by a rooting hormone. My grandmother rooted cuttings of various plants, and merely used a tea made from willow cuttings. I remember her saying "nothing roots like a willow branch." If you collect pussy willow branches in the spring, and put them in a jar of water, you will notice good roots on the stems in just a few days. My grandmother would merely collect a few willow branches, cut them into two inch pieces, split the pieces lengthwise with a knife and put them in a pail of water for a day or so, making a tea. She would then remove the willow pieces, soak her cuttings in the tea for a day before sticking the cuttings in soil and also use the diluted tea to water the cuttings.

In doing a little research on the matter, I learned that any kind of willow will work (any Salix species). Apparently the willow contains an acid which is natural rooting hormone, similar to the active ingredient in most rooting hormone products available commercially. I frankly tried this technique one time and it worked well. I expect it may be why my grandmother had such good success rooting her rose cuttings and other woody ornamentals.

Many vegetable gardeners have used teepee trellises for their pole beans. They can also work nicely for some annual flowering vines, such as clematis. The idea is to use generally straight wood poles, which may be collected from a woods. If you live in a big city, you may need to purchase the poles. The poles can be about an inch in diameter and tied at the top in the form of a tepee. It is easy to use just four poles arranged in a square at the ground and tied at the top. My grandmother 's technique, which I do not recall *ever* seeing elsewhere, was to use four poles about 7 or 8 feet long and tie them in the middle (about waist high) rather than at the top, and spreading the poles like a tepee. The extended parts of the poles above the tie provided an outwardly flaring support for the upper portion of the plants. She thought this was easier for picking, and also provided better sunlight and air ventilation. See page 65.

INSTALLING GARDEN POSTS

My grandmother was also fond of garden trellises for flowering vines, and she normally used naturally rot resistant poles from the farm woods, such as walnut or locust, to support the trellises. *Over* the years I have installed numerous posts in the garden, usually 4"x4" or 6"x6" redwood, cedar or treated lumber. My such poles were used for supporting trellises for vines, or for garden arches, arbor structures, large bird feeders, lights, etc.

Although not my grandmother's idea, I have found a rather easy and quick way to support posts in the ground for stability. Poured concrete around the posts may be the best plan, although it can limit the area available for planting near the posts. My technique is to use two cross pieces of lumber about 12 inches long made from rot resistant 2"x4", 2"x6", 1"x6", etc. They are securely screwed to the post with stainless or brass screws, one cross piece being near the bottom of the post and another on the opposite side of the post and located a few inches below the planned ground level. If the post is expected to receive pressure from all directions, cross pieces may also be used on all of the sides of the post. After a good back filling, stability for the post is provided in all directions. Hopefully, you also had a grandmother who passed along some of her older ideas or techniques, some of which are generation proof.

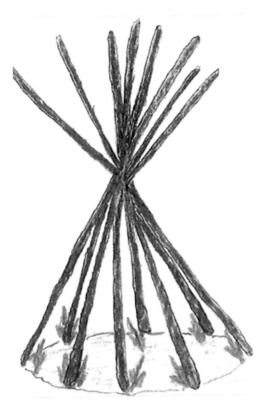

Teepee Trellis

Rose Jar

DEER CONTROL

The writer has learned about an electronic product for scaring deer and other animals from your garden. It is a battery operated pulsating impact water sprinkler head connected to a garden hose and activated by a motion detector. The product is Scarecrow Motion Activated Sprinkler, which has a very high satisfaction rating by customers.

The company manufacturing the product is Contech Electronics Inc., P.O. Box 115, Saanichton, BC, Canada, V8M 2C3. Telephone: 1-800-767-8658. Their website is www.scatmat.com.

The Scarecrow product detects animals that come within range and briefly squirts water from it's pulsating impact sprinkler head. The combination of sudden noise, motion and a jet of water startles the animals and they flee. The Scarecrow unit has a range of 35 feet and with it's 110 degree spread will reportedly protect up to 1,000 sq. ft. of garden.

The device is on a stake which is merely pushed into the soil at the desired location and connected to a garden hose. For best results, customers suggest moving it every few days so that the animals do not get used to it's location. It sells for $79.00 and has a two year warranty.

At our gardens in Golden Valley, Minnesota, we were always plagued by rabbits, groundhogs, and an occasional deer, and the Scarecrow product was very helpful. After using it, we seldom ever had an animal in the yard. We also had flower gardens at our home in Montana, with the same animal problems noted above, except we had more deer and an occasional moose or elk. Our gardens there were large and in widely separated areas, so we never tried the Scarecrow product.

We did try every known commercial deer repellent and many home remedies, but none of them worked to any extent. We even tried mountain lion urine, provided to me by a friend in Montana who used it some way in trapping fur-bearing animals. Don't ask me how he collected it. It did work for a day or so to scare away the deer and moose, but they soon figured out that there were no mountain lions around. It was very smelly and objectional to spray and even kept me away from the gardens for a few days. I also tried coyote urine but that was even less effective.

The Scarecrow product was also used by me at my home in Bonita Springs, Florida, to control numerous varmints, including rabbits, raccoons, skunks, foxes, fruit rats, opossums, groundhogs, and an occasional coyote. We had a lot of fruit trees, as well as easily accessible fruits such as pineapple, melons, grapes, blueberries, papaya and bananas. We also used it on our dock to keep birds from roosting on the boat.

There are also some chemicals which repel deer and other animals. These include Ropel animal and rodent repellent and Plantskydd deer repellent. I have not used them so don't know how dangerous they might be to children and pets.

MAKING A LARGE WREATH

One of the holiday decorations I have always favored is a nice evergreen wreath. Small wreaths are rather easy to make using a wire frame purchased from a garden center or hardware store. However, my family has always enjoyed a large wreath made for the outside of the home and displayed in a prominent location. Several years ago, I developed a simple and inexpensive way to make a wreath up to about five feet in diameter, and have often done so.

What I do is purchase a 4'x8' sheet of tempered 1/4" thick pegboard, or a half sheet if available. Pegboard has holes about an inch apart and is normally used with hangers or brackets for storing tools, etc. With pegboard one can make a wreath frame 48 inches in diameter. When fitted fully with evergreen branches, a nice wreath of about *five* feet diameter will be the result. Of course, a nice smaller wreath may be made also by using the inner portion of the pegboard removed when the large wreath frame is cut.

Anyway, my technique is to locate the center of the 4'x4' square piece of peg board before the inner portion is removed. This is done by using a straight piece of thin wood or a piece of angle iron, etc. laid from the opposite corners and marked with a short line, which when done both ways will give you a cross indicating the exact center. I drive a small nail at the center, then fasten a strong string or piece of wire to the nail and a pencil at the other end. Thus, the outer and inner edges of the frame may be scribed. For a frame of four foot size, I recommend the frame to be about 5 inches wide between the outer and inner edges, for strength. For smaller sizes, the frames may be of smaller width. While at it, I like to make the larger wreath, then one or two smaller ones cut from the inner portions of the frame material. An electric hand held jig saw is useful to cut the circle edges of the frames.

Any available evergreens may be used to complete the wreath. I prefer some type of fir, since the needles have rounded ends and are softer. Spruce needles are sharp and sticky and gloves need to be worn. I have also used arborvitae and scotch pine. When in Montana for the holidays, I use Douglas fir since such trees are abundant on my land. When in Florida, I prefer the beautiful Frazer fir. In Florida, I have found that the tree lots often give away the branches from pruned or poorly shaped trees, or sell bunches for a small sum.

In making the wreaths, I take four to six branches (depending on how full the foliage may be) about 12" to 18" long, place them together and arrange to make a nice bunch. I hold the bunch by one hand on top of the frame, and with the other hand wire the bunch to the frame, using some type of flexible wire. It helps to place the frame on a table or a couple of saw horses. Any wire may be used as long as it is flexible and strong enough to hold the bunches of evergreens. Cut a piece of wire about 8 to 10 inches long, bend it like a hairpin, place it over the branches, stick the wire ends through holes in the pegboard, and twist the wire ends tight underneath. With the wires tight underneath, one wire is normally adequate to hold the branches tight to the frame. Then, take another bunch and overlap the first bunch about a third to half, covering the first wire and the thicker branch ends. Proceed to place the bunches of branches around the entire frame. When you come to the last space, lift the ends of the first bunch and place the thick ends of the last bunch under the first one before wiring. A piece of wire may be fastened to the frame at the selected top, and a loop made in the wire for hanging the wreath over a nail or other fastener.

Additional decorations may be added, such as nice pine cones, berries, balls, ribbons, etc. My preference is to merely add a large red bow at the bottom, and tie some lights on top of the evergreens. I like a single color set of the smaller type lights, such as blue or white. After the season, merely cut and remove the wires and the greenery and store the frame for another year. In the writer's opinion, such a large lighted wreath near the garage or entrance to the home is quite attractive for the holiday season.

TOOLS AND EQUIPMENT

To garden effectively, numerous tools and equipment are needed by the gardener and workers. I was fortunate to acquire a few items from my father, but most of my tools for the garden (and wood working) have been acquired over the years. My theory has always been that you cannot do a good job without the right tools. Some of mine have come from garage sales, but most from local hardware stores. Listed below are my various tools.

Shovels, spades and forks
    preferably with long handles
Hoes
    combination hoe
    triangular hoe
    digging hoe
Edging tools
Rakes
    garden rake
    grass rake
    leaf rake
Garden knife
Hedge shears
Grass shears
Planting tools
    bulb planters
    seed savers
    dibbles
Wheel-barrow or Garden cart

Trowels
    planting trowel
    bulb trowel
    scoop trowel
Hand weeder
Cultivators
    manual with large prongs
    star-wheeled
Pruners
    hand pruner
    long-handled pruner
        tree pruner
        pruning saw
Plant supports
    hoops
    stakes
Labels
Hat and· gloves
Rain gauge

HOT SUMMERS

It seems that after some cool times in the spring of 2014, even in May, we in the northern climes can expect to experience a hot and dry summer, according to predictions. Our gardens always need some care, but with the hot days predicted for June through most of August for the next few years, taking care of the garden is an early morning endeavor. Also, we have to be thankful if we have some type of watering system for the garden and a timed sprinkler system for the lawn.

Last summer was hot in the northern areas, as well as most of the country, and the experts predicting the weather indicate that hot summers are to be the norm for some years. We continue to read about man-made global warming. I am not aware that man can change the weather, but various people predict an unusually warm summer this year and more to come. We do know that extremely warm summers are also being predicted this summer for various northern regions. Hopefully, last summer was not a preview of what to expect. We do know that Oklahoma and Texas set records last June, July and August for the for the hottest temps ever in recorded history.

One thing I was told by my mother was that the winter of 1935-36 was the coldest on record at that time, and the summer of 1936 was the hottest. I am not sure why she told me that information, but expect it may have had something to do with my birth.

With respect to last summer (2013), it was hot in July, good moisture in August, and cool in September. Various vegetables did rather well, as did the flowers in Minnesota.

Watering is particularly important during hot summers. Use enough water to wet the soil deeply at least once a week, rather than several light sprinklings. It is not good to apply too much water, which can be just as bad as too little moisture. For perennials, it is good to get the moisture down about 12" in the soil, once a week. Also, remember that very big differences of moisture in the soil can be quite harmful to plants, perhaps even more so than not enough water.

Applying a nice covering of mulch can also be quite helpful in reducing evaporation and also retaining moisture in the soil. Mulch is also good to control weeds and over time adds organic to the soil.

AUTUMN CLEAN-UP

As an optimist, autumn is not the end of the gardening year. Instead, it may be considered the beginning of next year's garden. Another thing to consider is that the cooler and crisp days of fall are good for working in the gardens. It is also a good time to think about changes or improvements in the gardens, such as modifying the shape of some of the gardens, and the placement of some of the perennials.

Clean up of the gardens is a particular requirement. Spent flowers should be removed, and all weeds should be pulled and discarded. After frost, the perennials should be cut back and any diseased ones removed and put in the trash (not composted).

Delphiniums, in particular, require some special autumn care. After they are done blooming, the flower spikes should be cut to just below the bottom florets. After frost, the stalks should be cut back to about 8 inches. A little mulch could be placed around the plants. However, if there are many trees on the property, my recommendation is to not add cover or mulch around the plants. The leaves from the trees will collect around the base of the delphs and provide sufficient cover for the winter.

Leaves, cuttings from perennials and pulled annuals may be added to the compost bin, but not any diseased ones. It is also good to mow the lawn and then rake and remove the the grass clippings and add the leaves and clippings to the compost. When this is done, the lawn should be sprayed for weeds. In the gardens, compost and gypsum should be placed in the spaces between the plants, and then the soil between plants should be spaded and permitted to break up over the winter. Also, the perennials and shrubs should be watered before the ground freezes.

As a final job, all garden tools should cleaned and stored for the winter. All plant supports, stakes, cages and trellises, etc. should also be removed and stored if they are so located so that they might be damaged by wind or snow over the winter. Any sculptures which could also be damaged should be covered for the winter. Finally, autumn is the time to clean all bird houses.

Best wishes for all your gardening and landscaping endeavors. Phil Smith

Printed in the United States
By Bookmasters